AF255509

Frank Walsh

INVESTING&TRADING STRATEGIES: TYPES OF INVESTMENT

A clear and comprehensive guide to the most essential and profitable forms of investment

Table of Contents

Introduction

They often say that to make a lot of money with investments, you need many millions. This, however, does not mean that to earn, you must always invest large sums. Even small investors can get great satisfaction from their investments: invest your money wisely. You can start with small amounts and then gradually grow, or you can remain a small investor and be content with your nest egg.

I've always said that every investor is a different story. Everyone must choose their path and follow their aspirations and adjust according to their resources and needs.

But what are the real opportunities that the market offers to the small amateur investor?

Investing can cover a wide range of options. One of the most traditional types of investing is in the stock market. This has long been seen by some as complex, significantly as the first form of investment, however, times are changing. The new generation of stockbrokers available online is already a clear demonstration that it is now easy (and relatively cheap) to get involved in buying and selling stocks even if you are not a professional.

If you are interested in trading stocks and shares yourself, then be aware that there is a risk involved: stocks can go down in value as well as - indeed - up. It is essential to investigate the market thoroughly before diving into buying, and you should see the stock market as a medium to long-term investment. If you invest intending to make a quick profit, then it is very likely that you will be disappointed.

Another type of investment, which has become particularly popular in recent times of profound market instability, is real estate, or bricks and mortar. Putting money into residential properties and then taking an income by renting them out is seen by many as a win-win situation. The biggest downside to this type of investment is that you will need a large sum of capital to get started, otherwise you will need to take out a large loan, which will need to be repaid.

Investing money or time in starting your own business, selling a product or service to make a profit is an indirect form of investment, alternative to financial investments. The same applies to investments in safe-haven assets, ranging from real estate to precious objects, to art, collections, etc... Even the latter can be considered an investment if the intention is to resell them to make a profit.

It is difficult to say how and why people make their investment decisions. It is also not true that investors are betting on the safe side every time. Speculating a higher-than-usual profit in the short term is a not too unusual trend, and I am not just talking about trading enthusiasts. Such kind of investment is classified in the jargon as "speculative". After all, many speculators in stocks and real estate have made a lot of money by taking huge risks.

It would be a waste of time to detail all types of financial or related investments available, as not all types of investments are interesting, especially for the small amateur investor.

In this manual, we will focus on the main and most representative ones.

So, if you are ready, I would say get going.

Chapter 1: Forex Trading

Technical Analysis of Forex Trading

When price patterns change from one to another, causing a change of prices in the market, these patterns have a specific way of doing so. When changes in price patterns in markets are studied and mastered to help in the prediction of future price patterns, this is now called the technical analysis. Most traders prefer using technical analysis over fundamental analysis. However, some traders use both the analysis techniques. Technical analysts use a different method to analyze the price patterns in markets. The techniques used include:

Chart Patterns

These are patterns where the prices are drawn on charts inform of graphs. When data is drawn on the graph, there is always a repetitive pattern. This pattern shows the movement of the prices in the forex markets. It shows the strength and the weakness of the trade. Some forex traders use the chart patterns as continuation signals or the reversal signals.

The continuous signals contain, triangle, flag and pennant, channel, and cup with the handle while the reversal includes, double top reversal, double bottom reversal, triple top reversal, head and shoulders and so many other. There are three groups of chart patterns that traders use — these chart patterns area the candlestick patterns, the harmonic patterns, and the traditional patterns.

The technical analysts using this chart patterns use horizontal lines, trend lines, and the Fibonacci retracement level to find the signals of the chart patterns. The chart patterns show the strengths and weaknesses of the forex market.

Horizontal Lines

These lines are also called sideways trends. These lines connect the lows and the highs in the variables. In this case the prices on the charts. These lines show the price that is below the support level and above the resistance level.

Trend lines

Trend lines are lines drawn on the chart or the graph to show support or resistance. These trend lines are dependent on the direction in which the prices are going in the forex trade. They are also known as horizontal support and resistance. When analysts are using trend lines in the chart patterns, they can see the increase or decrease in supply and demand.

The traders make up their mind whether to invest or not when this increase or decrease occur. When the prices are going up, it is called an upward trend, and the forex traders can sell. When the prices are going down, it is called a downward trend, and buyers can make their entry in the trade.

Fibonacci Levels

These levels in chart patterns exhume the hidden support and resistance. The support and resistance can be hidden due to the golden ratios. The origin pf Fibonacci is from the mathematical proportion, but it acts like the old support and resistance in the chart patterns when the price levels are laid out. The mathematical proportions used in this method is very different from the highs and the lows on the price charts.

Candlestick Patterns

Forex technical analysts use to find the open, high, and low-price levels in the markets (OHL). The prices sought must be of a specific period in the trading session so that a comparison of the trader's behavior during the trade is made against the prices at that particular time. This analysis will help in predicting the future price movement in the forex trade market.

Technical Analysis Indicators

The technical forex analysts use the price action indicator. These indicators include:

The moving average

The moving average indicator shows the averages of prices in a given period. The moving averages display the direction of the market. The moving average helps balance the prices in the market by removing the unwanted prices. This removal helps the trader focus on the trend of the prices in the market. There are four types of the moving averages, namely the exponential moving averages (EMA), simple moving averages (SMA), linear weighted average (LWA), and the smoothed averages.

Bollinger Bands

This indicator is a tool used in technical analysis that comprises of three lines. These lines are plotted positively and negatively but away from the simple moving average of the currency price. These lines are adjustable to the trader's preference. The Bollinger bands help measure the variation degree of prices during the trade. In simpler terms, it measures the volatility of the market in a given period.

Amongst the three lines in the Bollinger, the middle line shows the trend direction of the prices while the upper and lower lines are the volatility lines, also called the volatility bands. The upper and the lower bands are moved above and below the middle band by two standard deviations. This movement of the upper and the lower bands put the price between the two outside lines. This price does not stay here for a long time because it is always moving around the middle line.

The Moving Average Convergence Divergence (MACD)

This price indicator shows the momentum of the market. It shows when the market is doing well or not and the force behind this action. While using this indicator, a signal will always be evident is a market is moving in one direction. The Moving Average Convergence Divergence indicator belongs to a class of oscillators. Oscillators are technical indicators too and shown separately, below the prices in the charts.

This step-by-step guide will show you everything you need to know to enter, manage, and exit trades in Forex trading.

Entering

An easy way to start trading is by using a demo account. If you use forex demo software like FXCM, Interactive Brokers or MetaTrader you can trade with just one click. It's free to open a demo forex trade account in these three affiliates, and the funds are credited instantly. Don't forget that forex trading is a risky activity so always use discretion when investing your hard-earned money.

The procedure is very simple. Open your Forex demo account and make a single trade without setting stop loss points or taking any other measures!

Step 1: The "fundamental" of the trade

It's very important to understand the basic concept of risk management with forex trading. The fundamental character of a transaction in forex trading is the quantity of money you are risking on each side of the trade.

The fundamental quantity of money at stake in a currency exchange transaction is the number of pips (price interest points) that separate the current closing price (or bid) from where you want to buy the base currency and where you wish to sell the quote currency.

For example: If you buy EUR/USD at $1.1655, your point of entry is at 1.1655. If you sell EUR/USD at $1.1680, your point of exit is at 1.1680.

Step 2: The "objective" of the trade

The objective of a transaction in forex trading is the amount of money you risk on each side of the trade. For example: If you buy EUR/USD at $1.1655, your objective is to close at 1.1675 or above the current bid price (i.e., ensure that your stop loss has not been triggered). If you sell EUR/USD at $1.1680, your objective is to close at 1.1630 or below the current offer price (i.e., ensure that your stop loss has not been triggered).

Step 3: The "applied" risk management strategy

In order to stay safe and make reasonable profits you need to follow a sound risk management strategy. This is called applied risk management in forex trading. Applied risk management strategies are implemented just before you enter a trade, or just after you enter a trade, but before the trade is closed.

Step 4: Entering the "trade"

You must enter a trade if you think that there will be a change in the current price trend. Essentially, entering a trade means forecasting that there will be an increase or decrease in demand for the currency pair you are trading. Forex traders spend countless hours studying charts and previous market activity to build predictive models that will allow them to forecast price behavior.

If your forecast is correct, you will likely close a winning position and the profits will be taken out of the current position. This will mean that your stop loss has been triggered, as you are required to exit the trade at a specified price.

If it's not correct, you will want to take a profit and that means you would have to close your losing position on the contrary by taking out part of your losses (i.e., execute a take profit order).

Winning Strategies:

1.Forex intraday trading strategy

The rate of the day is not subject to major changes. But there is always deformation. It can occur in the event and odd months: increases, decreases, stays on an unchanged level, moves to the opposite direction. So, on a daily basis the rate of the day will be characterized by such deviations which you need to take into account, if you want to make profitable entry and exit points for a trade. There is a loss of the price in the intraday trading strategy which means that you should enter into a new trade only after recovery, because if the rate will drop, you lose money from the previous trade. It is better to trade longer term intraday strategy.

The following may be considered as a specific feature of intraday trading:

This feature determines that the open position should be closed at minor changes in position during the course of day. Otherwise, if the price continues to move in the same direction, then deviation will become greater.

2. Long-term trading strategy

The purpose of this strategy is to know where the trend moves and how it is going to develop further, and using time features: "the trend is your friend." This strategy requires a large amount of money for making a trade. It is based on high probability and profit potential. When you are in a trade, you can stay within it for several weeks. The term of the investment is estimated in the terms of weekly and monthly cycles, and even years. They give a chance to trade tendencies which were formed for a long time.

3. Forex intraday scalping strategy

It is used by those who trade currencies from home with small amounts of capital. The intraday scalping strategy is based on the practice of opening and closing position within a few hours. The main objective of this type of trading is to quickly make profits as high as possible, and then to get out quickly.

4. Trading strategy by copy traders

This strategy is characterized by the fact that its main focus is not on entering and leaving positions but on determining the location of currencies in the time frame set up by the copy trader. The main trading instruments include the Forex pairs with the primary indicators such as candles, moving averages, Ichimoku, Fibonacci, etc.

5. Forex swing trading strategy

The main goal of this strategy is to make money on the rise and fall. The goal is to enter a trade using a "set-up". After that you wait until the second period opens and close its position. In the meantime, you do not touch anything.

Chapter 2: Long Term Trading

In any business, the first step is knowing your customer. Long-term traders are different from short-term day traders in many respects: they typically keep positions open for days, weeks, months or even years; they're more focused on trading companies than trading stocks; they are less concerned with making money on each trade and more determined to make money as a whole.

But one thing that all short-term traders have in common: they trade based on rumors, rumor has no cost. It's not only the cost of the transaction but also the time involved in making a decision whether to enter a position or not. Many long-term traders turn down very good trades because they didn't trust their "gut feeling" that something was wrong with the market.

Long-term traders are by nature risk takers; once you understand why, you'll find it easier to trade futures and options.

What are rumors? Rumors are what you don't hear, but should. They're opinions that you might hear from other traders that you should consider before trading. Much of the information we process when we trade comes from rumors: we see some technical analysis chart pattern and assume that a stock is going to bounce off it, or we pick a good setup based on price action and volume. You can get very rich on the wrong side of a rumor (just ask Nynex traders who lost $10 million in July 1995). The key to trading is to use rumors (information) in your favor.

1. Trading Plan

There are two kinds of traders in the market: those who trade with a plan and those who do not. The ones with a plan have a much higher success rate than the ones without one, regardless of how well that person knows what they're doing. If you don't have an up-to-date trading plan, you'll trade for the sake of trading for the sake of trading. You'll make some small profits along the way and get discouraged when it doesn't continue.

There are many ways to write a winning trading plan: online, paper, computerized... any one of them is fine. But one thing is for sure: when you write it down on paper and check your plan against the market, it will be of great help to you.

2. Money Management

Money management is critical to your trading success. It's important that every trader keeps discipline in their trading; in other words, they shouldn't trade emotional because they are losing money all the time and they keep breaking their rules. You must have a plan, and once you set your plan, stick to it. A trader's psychology is much stronger than that of an average person. When we're losing money, we blame the market – or ourselves – for the loss. When we win, we go into a trading frenzy with no fear of picking winners and losers.

We're all human after all; money management is not just about keeping losses under control but about keeping profits on track as well.

3. Risk and Money Management

The essence of risk management is to know your position and protect your capital by taking off a small part of your winning position or add a small part of your losing position. Many traders do not like to take a loss; they keep holding on to their loser hoping that it will come back. That's why they lose money in the first place! This is why you must protect your capital by keeping losses small.

4. Trading Psychology

Your trading psychology is a very important part of trading. If your profitability is below 80%, it's time to change your mindset; instead of trading, start thinking about it. What do these four statements have in common? They all say the same thing: "I'm losing money. I have to change something." You should ask yourself: am I losing money because I am a bad trader or because the market is bad?

TIP: When trading with real money, keep your initial capital at 25% of the sum you actually have. For example, if you have $100,000, start out with $25,000. This is not a small sum of money. If you're a good trader and manage that $25,000 well (don't let it go up to $50 or $60K), then you can invest another 25%, and so on. If you're a bad trader and lose that $25K, you may lose a lot more.

Strategies: buy and hold strategy in long term trading advice.

The buy and hold strategy is an excellent way to make consistent profits without risking a lot of money at once. A trader will usually look at the charts for a period of two to three weeks and decide if they think the trend will continue or they should take some profits. Once they have decided, they enter long positions for their profit objectives. The buy and hold trader looks for stocks that are strong (i.e. have a good trend) and are not too expensive. The trader should only choose stocks that are in their favor, i.e. have a strong trend and lots of good news.

in short term trading advice, buy and hold strategy is best used in intraday market conditions where the broker's volatility spreads themselves in order of price movement distance from the average movement (value line). Following such strategies will make the most profit and increase the trade to a level of risk for the trader's performance (the money they can afford to risk).

The buy and hold strategy is a long-term trading strategy that can be extremely effective if done correctly, but it has its shortcomings as well. The main reason the buy and hold strategy is so effective is because the trader will only sell when they have reached their target, which is usually a significant price increase or move in the upward direction (depending on what type of stocks you are looking for). This strategy is usually best used with smaller stocks that settle in the over-the-counter sector.

The buy and hold strategy can be very profitable, but it is also risky because of the time frame required to see results. It's easy to say that you are going to hold onto a stock that has tremendous potential for 5 years, but in reality, it can be very difficult to do so if you've only invested a small amount of money. For this reason, traders must always have an exit strategy ready. It's also the reason why some traders have a portfolio of stocks that they are ready to sell if one begins to fail or is about to fail.

The best advice for long term traders is to never take on more risk than you can afford, be patient, and always have a profit target in mind. These are just some of the many tricks that long term traders use day in and day out.

The buy and hold strategy in short term trading is not the same as the buy and hold strategy for long term trading. The two strategies are very different, because the short-term trader can only withstand losses for a certain amount of time. This makes the buying and selling more difficult to do at times. If you are trying to trade a stock that has no news, is doing nothing, or doesn't have potential for a significant price increase you will be able to hold onto that stock without problems.

Chapter 3: Stock Trading

1. An investor should always keep an eye on the money that flows in and out of their trading account.

2. When trading in shares, an investor should also make sure they don't overtrade or invest more than they can afford to lose.

3. While shares share ownership, a company's performance is heavily influenced by its management and leadership team, so investors need to be wary of share prices that fluctuate too much due to temporary factors such as market news.

4. Know the fundamentals of the security that you are investing in. Understanding the stocks' technical structure can help inform your investment decisions and increase your overall return. For example, it is easier to trade stocks with share prices that are high relative to the company's size as compared to large companies where shares trade at a premium to their fair value margin.

5. Always pay attention to the intrinsic value of a company compared to its share price. Investing in a company's stock based on its popularity rather than its fundamentals can lead to poor investment decisions and missed opportunities.

6. As an investor, it is important not only to keep close track of your trading account but also any companies that you are invested in. If you are not sure whether an investment is a good one, then stop trading and research the security before buying it.

7. If you are new to the stock market, you should start by trading in blue chip stocks with a strong transparency and reporting record.

8. Using Stop Loss Order can help your security investment performance from suffering big losses.

9. Stock Exchange is Market where dealers buy and sell stocks, it's a marketplace for the buyers and sellers to trade securities back and forth with each other through a broker.

10. Margin Trading is trading with money borrowed from a broker and using it to buy securities. Margin trading is carried out in a margin account. A margin account must be kept open for this kind of trading (Securities and Exchange Commission [SEC] 2006).

Here are the four basic trading strategies that you should investigate. They all involve subsidiary strategies. There is a lot of confusion regarding these strategies because a lot of people use different labels for them, but I have simplified them as much as possible into four different types. Many of these come under fancy names but focus on what you are actually doing. That is how I have classified these strategies to make them as clear as possible.

It is also important to understand that regardless of the strategy that you employ; in addition, you must do proper analysis. Analysis is what will make or break these strategies. These strategies can help you achieve your financial goals on a day-to-day basis or a long-term basis only if you do the proper analysis.

Chapter 4: Swing Trading

Swing trading involves buying stock in a company and waiting between two to six days to a couple of weeks for that stock to reach its full potential. If you are short selling the stock, its fullest potential for you, at least, is when it crashes to a very low level. Once it reaches a target point, you then exit the stock. Swing traders normally put in a good-until-canceled order.

For example, based on technical analysis, a stock is showing a lot of volume, and it is meeting a lot of resistance at 30. Based on volume analysis, it seems like people are buying more and more into the stock, and the volume is increasing tremendously. In this situation, I would then put in a good-until-canceled buy limit order for any price above $30. Sure enough, a lot more investors plow into the stock, and the stock goes past the $30 resistance level, and I lock at $30.25. It then hits $31 and there is a pullback to $29.

A swing trader would wait several days or even a couple of weeks until the stock reaches a profitable point or to maximize opportunity costs; the trader leaves the stock at a slight loss. Whatever the case may be, swing trading involves taking a position only to the point where the stock reaches your target appreciation, and you automatically exit. Swing traders can utilize technical stock analysis using volume and price fluctuations, or they can employ stock value analysis by paying attention to things like the revenue of the company, competitive position, industry position as well as prospective developments in the news that might impact the company's stock performance. Regardless of the analysis that they used, swing traders pursue a strategy where they will remain parked in the stock for enough time to see a nice swing up or a nice swing down.

Chapter 5: Position Trading

A position trader is somebody who will buy a position in a company for the long term. By long term, we are talking about several months to even years. The position trader is not really worried about the short-term fluctuations of the stock. This type of strategy does not rely on trends or market fluctuations in terms of the company's particular evaluation. Instead, the position trader uses a strategy that smoothes out whatever near-term price volatility may be. The key to success in position trading is a fairly long-term yet steady rate of appreciation.

For example, if your end goal is to protect your money's value against inflation and taxes, then your strategy would be to take the rate of inflation as well as your desired growth rate and use that as your ROI benchmark. You do this, of course, with the understanding that taxes will be taken up. So, a position trader then would look at the beginning the year when they bought the position and at the end of the year where they are still hanging on to the stock. If they see that there is a nice percentage increase in ROI, compared to inflation and other factors; afterward, they consider their trade successful.

Usually, position traders would not just measure their success against inflation because, let us face it, for the past decade, inflation has been very, very low. In fact, it is abnormally inferior by historical standards. It is so low that it is kind of scary if you ask me.

Instead, the position trader would factor in opportunity costs. An opportunity cost is obviously defined as the value of alternative investments. Put simply, if you did not invest in this stock and chose to invest in another stock instead, how would your current stock measure up? That is when you know whether you left a lot of money on the table, or you are actually doing quite well because alternative stocks are not doing that great. Position traders use the Dow Jones Industrial index or some sort of index to determine the relative health of their portfolio. If they notice that the rate of appreciation of their portfolio keeps up with the rest of the market, then they consider themselves successful.

Chapter 6: Day Trading

Given the wide variety of stocks to trade, day trading in stocks is particularly common among beginners, but not because it is easy (far from it), but because it gives a feeling of greater risk control. Typically, in the stock market, positions are closed out at the end of the day to avoid the 'gapping risk' that occurs when the stock price at market opening is significantly lower or higher than the previous day's price, due to unexpected news or events that occurred overnight.

Understanding day trading also means understanding and using stock indices to measure market performance. This data is important because it can affect, as is often the case, the price of trades you want to make or have made. On the other hand, all stocks fluctuate, and changes can be recorded not only on a daily basis but also throughout the year.

Chapter 7: Value Investing

Value investing is also known as the Warren Buffett strategy or buy and hold. Value investing boils down to buying stock that the market has somehow someway overlooked. What you are doing is you are looking at a company that is in a really good position and should be valued more by the stock market. For whatever reason, its stock price is, in your opinion, below its full value in the future.

This is how Warren Buffet became a multibillionaire many times over. He has this uncanny ability of looking at certain companies that may be trading at a very high price already but looking at their balance sheet as well as their industry positioning and the health of the US or global economy several years down the road and using these pieces of information to make stock purchase decisions. Obviously, he is doing something right because he has become one of the wealthiest people on the planet using this strategy.

It is important to understand that value investing does not necessarily mean you buy a company which has a stock price that seems stuck. Ideally, that would be the best.

However, value investing also means paying top dollar for a company that is trading at a decent level now with the confidence that price is going to go much higher in the future. You then buy the stock, and you hold onto it for a long period of time. Your success meter factors in several years of appreciation.

As you can already tell, swing trading and day trading tend to go hand in hand. Position trading and value investing tend to go hand in hand as well. These four strategies differ from each other, but these two pairings involve quite a bit of similarity. Again, when picking a trading strategy, make sure you factor in what makes sense to you, your needs, your immediate and midterm financial goals as well as your risk appetite and risk profile.

Chapter 8: Understanding and Investing in Bonds

If you have an investment portfolio, there's a good chance that some of your holdings are in bonds. But if you're not sure what bonds are, how they work, or how you can learn more about them, don't worry! We'll answer the most common questions and get you up to speed with this basic introduction to understanding and investing in bonds.

What is a bond?

A bond is basically like getting an IOU from the government (or another entity). The entity creates a document stating that it owes someone X dollars on Y date. When the entity pays back what it owes at maturity date (which could be any time over 20 years), it pays back with interest.

What is the government selling bonds for?

The government's main reason for selling bonds is to raise money for various projects. They sell bonds at a set rate of interest to investors, who receive periodic interest payments and then get paid back with the principal when the bond matures.

When is the government going to start paying back what it owes?

The government usually sells bonds with a maturity of 10 years or less. Of course, that means that if you buy a 30-year bond, you'll be getting your principal back when you're in your 50s.

How do I know that the government is really going to pay me back?

You can think of bonds as similar to what happens when you buy a house. The bank will lend you the money, but it will use your house as collateral. If you don't pay the money back, the bank can foreclose and take your house. Similarly, if a country doesn't pay its bondholders back, or only pays them back with another bond (called a "debt swap"), there are consequences. Because bonds are traded on exchanges (like stocks), their value changes based on supply and demand and interest rates. If a government makes bondholders wait too long to get their principal back, they can ask the government for a lower interest rate. This means that the government will pay less interest, and that is one way that it can be forced to pay back its debt at a faster rate.

How does this affect me?

If you buy a bond (and there are many different kinds of bonds), you would collect interest on your investment from the entity that owes you money. You'll get paid at regular intervals (every 6 months in the case of US treasury bonds), and when the bond matures, you would get back your principal (again, this could be ten years in the future).

How do I buy a bond?

If you'd like to be an investor in bonds, you need to do two things. First, you need to decide which country or entity you want to be invested in. This is called making a "country allocation." In the US, bonds can be bought at your local bank or at any brokerage. They can also be traded on exchanges like stocks (for example, you could buy IBM bonds and sell Apple bonds). Bonds pay interest every 6 months (or other regularly occurring intervals).

What are my options for investing in bonds?

There are many kinds of bonds with different payouts and risks associated with them. Depending on your goals and risk tolerance, you might want to choose different types of bonds.

US Treasury Bonds (often called T-Bonds) are considered very low risk. They have a "AAA" rating and are backed by the US government. This means that if the entity that owes you money (the US government) falls behind in payment, the US will step in to pay its bondholders. T-bonds are easy, safe investments but pay low interest rates.

Corporate bonds (corporate IOUs) have a lower risk than T-bonds because corporations will not be bailed out by the government if they fall behind on their payments. However, their risk is still higher than T-bonds. Their interest rates are higher as well.

Municipal bonds are issued by state and local governments, and they're considered to have the lowest risk of default of any bonds because the entities that issue them can always raise taxes if they need more money. They pay lower interest rates than corporate bonds but higher interest rates than T-bonds.

As you can see, there are many different kinds of bonds, with a wide range of risks and potential returns associated with each kind of bond. Luckily, there are financial advisors that can help you sort through the options available to find ones that work for you and your goals.

Government Bonds:

Bonds issued by the federal government are called government bonds and are considered to be risk-free investments. Unlike corporate bonds, government bonds don't have any credit risk attached to them because you know that the issuer is guaranteed by the federal government. Bonds issued by corporations, on the other hand, can default and usually do so without any warning! Because of this higher credit risk, corporate bonds offer a higher yield than their safer counterparts.

Corporate Bonds:

Corporate bonds are debt securities issued by companies (rather than governments) to borrow money from investors at a future date with an agreement to pay out at least some interest over time and then repay the principal amount borrowed at maturity. The borrower pays the lender an interest rate that is set at the time of issuance based on the creditworthiness of the company. The riskier the company, or lower its credit rating, the higher (or "riskier") a yield you can expect from buying that company's bonds.

Corporate bonds are generally much more volatile in value than government bonds due to their higher risk, however they offer higher yields as well.

Corporate Bonds also trade actively on what's known as the "secondary market" while Government Bonds are traded mostly on what's known as the "primary market.

The most common way to purchase bonds is through brokerage accounts. There are several large brokerages which cater to individual investors, making it easy to place trades for as little as a few hundred dollars. Some brokerages even have minimums as low as $1 for bond trades.

The other way to invest in bonds is through mutual funds that invest in corporate and government bonds. Investors can buy into these funds with just a few hundred dollars. The fees associated with mutual funds, however, take away from any returns on your investment in the fund. These fees can eat away at the gains you make on the investment and may even make it unprofitable in some cases.

There are many types of bonds (corporate, government) that may be worth considering for investment. For example, US Savings Bonds are issued by the US Treasury. These bonds pay a fixed interest rate every six months until they mature on 30 years from the issue date. Some Savings Bonds may be cashed in before maturity, but at a steep loss as compared to what could have been earned had the full term been held to maturity.

Corporate bonds come in many different types of ratings and price points. High-quality corporate bonds that carry high credit ratings from Standard & Poor's or Moody's are usually considered to be safer than lower credit rated corporate bonds. The lower the credit rating, also known as the corporate bond's "credit spread", the higher the yield an investor may expect to receive.

The greater the risk, however, is usually accompanied by a greater expected return. High-risk bonds (i.e.: junk bonds) can pay double-digit yields but also have a high likelihood of default. The online bond calculator on this page allows you to quickly enter different parameters and scenarios and see how they affect your bond investment.

This is the perfect time to learn about bonds--because know-how could save you a boat load of money! Read on to find out when it makes sense, and when it doesn't, to invest in bonds.

Bonds are for more than just old people: they can be used strategically by young people too. They provide a tax benefit and can be a good way to diversify your portfolio. But before you buy any bonds, there are some things you need to know. Bonds are not all the same--there is a difference between "securities" and "obligations," with securities being riskier than obligations. Plus, there are short-term bonds and long-term bonds, and how you choose to use these will affect your return.

Since bonds do not have the same liquidity as stocks, you need to know when is a good time to buy them--and when it's not. You also need to have an understanding of how bond prices are determined--and this understanding can only come from practice and experience. Most importantly, you must learn the basics of portfolio construction so that you can determine the appropriate mix of stocks and bonds for yourself. This means learning about risk assessment, asset allocation, diversification, and more.

"The market value of a bond depends on several factors: the maturity, the coupon rate, and most importantly--the credit rating. Yield to maturity determines the approximate price at which a security will trade in the open market." Also called interest-rate characteristics, yield to maturity tells us how much interest investors will receive before the bonds reach full maturity date. The more risk you are willing to take, the higher the bond yield will be.

The price of a bond is determined by its coupon rate and the yield to maturity. The price of a bond goes up as its yield goes down (or conversely, as its price goes up as its yield goes down). Trading volume and volatility also affect the bond's price. If there is an uncertainty about the payment of interest or principal amount at maturity, then bonds are less likely to be traded for their full value. This uncertainty usually results from a lower rating or from a high degree of financial leverage in the issuing firm (i.e., after-tax profit less total interest expense divided by gross debt equals 5%). The value of a bond increases when its duration is reduced.

A bond's maturity date determines the length of time that you are investing in the debt obligations of an entity. Bonds have a place in every portfolio, given that they offer tax advantages and interest income. When bonds are used as a short-term financial instrument, then they should seek capital gains and return on investment (ROI).

Bonds are also used as part of the asset allocation process among investors; however, this type of strategy can lead to losses if the investor is not knowledgeable about these instruments. Bonds are also used as a longer-term investment and are particularly useful as a way to diversify one's portfolio. This kind of bond is used when an investor is concerned about the liquidity of the stock market. These bonds move in the opposite direction of stocks and provide an investor with an additional form of diversification. When short-term interest rates increase, then long-term interest rates usually increase correspondingly. Bond prices and yields move inversely to one another given that bonds are traded through yield.

Chapter 9: Understanding and Investing in Stocks

If you're looking for advice on how to invest your money, stocks are an excellent place to start. Read on and we'll break down the basics of how stocks work and how they can help grow your money -- if done right.

There are a lot of factors that come into play when investing in stocks, but one thing is clear: if you want to make a profit, you need to be willing to take risks. The more risk you're willing to take the higher your chance of making a profit will be - but with high-risk comes the possibility of losing it all. So where should you set that balance between risk and reward? That's something only you can decide by evaluating your own goals and limits.

Stocks are a type of financial instrument, and when you invest in them, you're buying shares of ownership in a company. You may not have heard of many of the companies we'll talk about here, but they employ thousands of people and make products that you consume every day.

In fact, it's possible that the companies on our list are even part of your portfolio already!

When you buy a share or stock in a company, there are two things at work: company earnings or profits, and the value (or price) that the market places on these profits. What are earnings? Well, they're simply what the company makes selling its products -- think about how much profit any store owner makes by selling shoes. This is company earnings.

Now, the other factor involved in buying a stock is what the market will pay for these profits. What does that mean? When you buy a stock, you are effectively agreeing to pay a certain price for the portion of ownership that you are purchasing. The market dictates how much your stock is worth based on how profitable that company is and how much investors think its profits will increase (or decrease) in the future. Today, we'll focus on earning potential and growth so that we can better understand how you make money with stocks.

We'll also discuss the ways to invest in stocks. It's important to understand that you're not always going to buy a full share of stock, but rather a small percentage. In fact, most stocks are broken down into two or more shares for every one sold!

You've probably heard of people "diversifying" their portfolios. This means that rather than putting all of your eggs in one basket -- or investing in just one type of stock -- you're spreading out your money. When you diversify, you are offering yourself options so that if the company whose stock you bought has a rough quarter (or year), your portfolio won't become immediately worthless. To diversify, invest in stocks from a variety of companies in different sectors.

Also, remember that there are two ways to invest: you can buy your stock and hold it (often referred to as "holding" the stock), or you can trade your stock (this is referred to as "trading" the stock). Once you've decided whether or not you want to buy or sell your stocks, you'll need to decide how you're going to buy them. There are a lot of ways to do this, but today we'll focus on just three: You can buy stocks online (or "online trading"), on the phone with a broker or adviser who works with an online trading service, or from the company itself directly.

If you're buying online, you have several options. You can peruse a stock market index to see which stocks are doing well and include them in your portfolio. Or you can look up individual stocks that interest you, or search for the most profitable stocks of the past 12 months.

Buying with a broker is a different story. You'll be paying a fee to get advice on which stocks you should be buying, and possibly also advice on how best to trade those shares if things don't go according to plan. Brokers can help you if you want to buy shares in a company that isn't actively trading online, or if you want to buy shares of a stock that's traded on a foreign exchange.

If you're looking to invest directly with the company, it's often a good idea to search for its financial information in advance so that you know exactly how much your investment is worth. You'll also need to decide whether or not you want your shares in common, preferred or limited form. Here are the differences:

Common Stock: This is the most traditional type of stock and it's generally worth more when the company is doing well. Many professional investors prefer to buy this stock because it's liquid (i.e., easy to sell and usually not restricted in any way).

Preferred Stock: This is debt that the company owes you, but with a couple of big exceptions. The company isn't legally obligated to pay your dividends until they have paid off their debt, so your money is at risk until that time comes. Also, when the company goes bankrupt, you will be paid before those with common stock -- but after those with bonds or preferred debt.

Limited Stock: This is a hybrid between preferred and common stocks, as it offers some of the benefits of both while keeping some of the risks (and potential rewards) associated with each type. There is much less of this type of stock available than the other two, but it can be a good choice if you like the company and want to invest in its future.

Now let's walk through the process and pick an investment. We'll assume that you've already determined how much money you want to spend on this move and that your preferred investment method is buying online with a broker. This gives us four choices: researching to pick an individual stock on your own, looking at a stock market index (like the Dow Jones or S&P 500), checking out a list of the most profitable stocks from one year ago, or searching for the most profitable stocks of all time. Most professional investing advice will point you towards the stock market index and picking from there, as this is almost guaranteed to be a safe investment.

When should you be buying stocks? And when should you be selling them? These are questions most investors ask themselves at some point in their investing careers. You'll often hear people say that timing the market is impossible, but that's not true. There are certain times of the year when stocks perform better than others, and there are many reasons why this is so.

If you're a value investor, you look for stocks with a low price / book value ratio and/or a low price / earnings ratio. These are the kind of companies that usually outperform the general market. But simply buying these stocks doesn't guarantee you'll make money. When you buy a stock, your return is directly related to how much money is made by the company. This in turn depends on when is the right time of year to buy stocks.

Stock prices fluctuate throughout the year, but it's not random. Stock markets tend to perform better during specific periods of the year, and this has been proven by numerous studies over many years around the world. For example, stocks in the United States tend to perform better from October through April. This is known as the October Effect. The reason for this is that people look to rebalance their portfolios in December after all their summer spending, and they like to buy stocks when there's more money in the market. That means demand is high for stocks which improves their price performance.

There's also an August Effect when people sell stocks at the end of summer, but it's nowhere near as strong as the

October Effect. Other studies show that stock markets tend to perform better during certain months of the year, and it has even been proven that day trading can be profitable during these periods with good software. So, it's possible to pick the best times of the year to buy stocks.

But here's the real question... Is it worth doing? Some people say that timing the market is worth the effort while others argue it's a waste of time. I say it depends on your investment style. If you're a value investor, then I recommend looking at historical stock trends and trying to time you're buying accordingly. After all, if you can get better performance without much risk with very little work, then why not? This way of investing is called passive investing and has been around for a long time. It's the basis of many investment strategies like dollar cost averaging. It's also very simple and easy to understand, which is why so many people use it even though so few people actually succeed.

When not to buy stocks

If you're not a value investor, then timing your stock purchases is probably a waste of time. If the prices are high, don't buy the stocks because you think they'll go even higher. Buying high and selling low isn't smart investing. It's gambling and the odds are against you. Don't try to time the market by buying at the lowest prices because that seldom works out well either unless you know what you're doing and have an edge in trading like day traders do. When in doubt, the middle ground is always the best choice. That's the way the average investor should play it, because if you're not a value investor and you try to time your stock purchases too much, then you're likely to lose money rather than gain it.

The bottom line is that timing your stock purchases can help your returns in some cases, but other times it actually hurts them. You can't predict with certainty when a stock will do well or when it will fall in price, so don't try to time your purchasing just for that reason. Instead, use good fundamentals and buy stocks with good prospects at reasonable prices. If you do that, then it doesn't really matter when you buy the stock. If you have a long-term horizon and you don't need to sell your stocks right away, then great! If not, then don't time your purchases and reduce your risk.

Chapter 10: Index and Mutual Funds: Why not?

An index fund is a group of securities that track the performance of an index. A mutual fund is a professionally managed investment company that pools money from many investors and invests it according to a specific strategy, objective or theme.

A mutual fund may invest in stocks, bonds, money market securities and other investments. An index fund generally tries to match the performance of its benchmark index such as the S&P 500 Index or Wilshire 5000 Index which means investing in all stocks in these indices to replicate their composition and return. By investing in all the companies within the index, an index fund takes advantage of diversification which reduces risk and increases return.

Both mutual funds and index funds are managed investment vehicles. Both types of funds offer investors a convenient way to pool their money for investing in securities. Mutual funds have professional management while index funds typically do not. Mutual funds are subject to regulatory oversight and must file annual reports with the SEC, provide semi-annual reports to shareholders, file periodic shareholder reports with the SEC, provide audited financial statements every year and more. Mutual fund shares can only be purchased through a financial professional or an online broker.

Both mutual funds and index funds are available as "open-end" investment companies or "closed-end" investment companies. Open-end investment companies add to their capital by continually offering shares to the public for purchase.

Both mutual funds and index funds provide investors with diversification by investing in hundreds or thousands of securities within their respective indices or asset categories. A mutual fund may offer exposure to securities from all over the world or in specific areas such as technology, healthcare, energy and more. An index fund typically does not have the ability to invest in securities outside of its specific index. This limits the risks and rewards experienced by investors.

Mutual funds and index funds are both very tax efficient. Both types of investments may generate capital gains when securities held within the fund are sold for a profit. Both types of funds can benefit from lower taxes by holding their investments within tax-advantaged accounts while waiting to sell other holdings or when redeeming shares into cash (see Taxes on Mutual Funds).

No-load mutual funds do not charge an up-front commission when shares are purchased directly from the fund company or through an online broker (see No-load Fund). Some mutual funds charge a deferred sales charge if shares are redeemed within a certain period after the purchase date (see Load Fund).

Both open-end mutual funds and closed-end index funds can be traded on an exchange at any time. Index funds within the same group (e.g., Vanguard 500 Index Fund, Vanguard Mid-Cap Index Fund) may be bought and sold at any time even though they have different net asset values (NAVs). Most mutual fund families allocate shares to investors on a pro rata basis each day based on the investor's account balance.

The number of index funds available is much larger than the number available for mutual funds. In addition to specialized indexes such as an international index or a small-cap index there are more general purpose broad market indexes such as the Russell 2000, S&P 500, Wilshire 5000 and Dow Jones Industrial Average. All of these indexes are tracked by corresponding mutual funds. The size and scope of these indices continually change and it is not uncommon for several new index funds to be launched while other existing index funds are closed or merged with other related index funds.

In theory, stock and bond market exchange prices can move faster than an individual investor's ability to execute transactions over multiple security types within a portfolio. For instance, an investor may wish to sell some bonds and purchase more stocks based upon a change in market conditions. With a mutual fund, investors can accomplish this by selling the bonds and buying the new stocks with a single transaction rather than selling one security then purchasing another separately. The individual investor can use an index fund alone or in combination with other investment strategies such as stock investing, bond investing and money market investing.

Index Fund Investing is the practice of utilizing index funds to build a diversified portfolio of securities for investment purposes.

The benefits of index fund investing are:

Because no active (human) decision making is involved in maintaining the portfolio, costs are low relative to actively managed funds. Actively managed funds depend on a manager to make buying and selling decisions in an attempt to outperform their chosen benchmark index. This can be costly, as the fund manager receives a percentage of asset under management each year. For example, an actively managed fund might charge a 1.5% annual management fee whereas an index fund may charge close to or less than .20%, and some indices like the S&P 500 are even free to invest in passively. In addition, there is still the cost of trading which will come out of your pocket every time you buy or sell a security in your portfolio.

Another cost associated with actively managed mutual funds is the Bid–ask spread. This is the amount of money it costs to get in and out of a position quickly. An index fund has no management to make buying or selling decisions so there aren't any trading costs associated. The Bid–ask spread varies across investment products and markets, but an average study found that this spread averaged between 1/2% to 1% per trade, meaning it costs more to trade with an actively managed mutual fund than an index fund.

An index fund investor doesn't have to worry about what the stock market will do; the indices or indexes they're investing in are designed to track the overall performance of an index like the S&P 500 or various sectors of the economy. The investor also doesn't have to worry about picking stocks or companies that may be losing money. The value of an index fund's investment is based on the value of all the holdings in that index, so if a company loses money it won't affect your portfolio's performance.

If you have a need to invest in the stock market but do not feel comfortable picking stocks or trading options, then there is no better way to invest than via mutual funds.

In order to buy and sell index funds or mutual funds it does require that you have an account with a broker such as TD Ameritrade, TD Trade King, E*Trade, Scottrade and so on. Mutual fund investing is best for beginners who don't want to worry about economic events that affect stocks and might lose money if they became emotional during times like these. Buying into mutual funds are great for many investors to start off with because if they don't have time to do the research and buy stocks then investing in mutual funds can diversify their portfolio of stocks and help them feel more comfortable.

When buying an index fund or a mutual fund there are three different types to choose from. The first type is called an "open-ended" fund which means that anyone can buy and sell at any time during the day however those who buy or sell on the open market will not receive as favorable of a price as those who invest directly from the company's website. The second type is called a "closed-ended" fund which means that they only offer a limited number of shares. Once these shares have sold, which can take days or even weeks, the fund will no longer allow anyone to buy into it. The third and best way to buy an index fund or mutual fund is called a "no-load" fund. A no-load fund is exactly what it says, you will NEVER pay any fees to invest in this specific mutual fund. Those who invest in a no-load index fund or mutual fund will receive the same price that the company receives for selling shares.

One very important thing to realize is that it takes money to make money. It doesn't make any sense to buy an index fund and hold onto it for ten years if you are not going to reinvest any of the gains from your initial investment into more shares of the same mutual fund. Therefore, it is a good idea to invest enough money in an index fund or mutual fund so that you can purchase additional shares every time you have excess capital since no one can predict what the stock market will do over a long period of time.

There are different types of index funds and mutual funds to invest in. The first type is called an "Index Fund" which tracks an index such as the S&P 500, Dow Jones 30

Industrial Average or the NASDAQ Composite. These funds will hold every single stock that is in the index which means that it diversifies your holdings by spreading your money across thousands of stocks. This is one of the most important factors of a mutual fund because just because one stock performed poorly over a period of time does not mean that every other stock in the index fund will do poorly as well. Therefore, since you are diversifying your holdings by buying thousands of different stocks with just a couple hundred dollars you will experience less volatility in your portfolio.

The second type of mutual fund is called a "Dividend Income Fund". These funds will invest in dividend paying stocks such as those which pay dividends to provide their investors with income. Usually, these funds will have a large portion of their holdings in utility companies, real estate companies and even some healthcare stocks.

The third type of mutual fund is called an "Active Management Fund" which means that the manager of the fund can make different types of investments other than buying all of the stocks in the index. The active management fund can also buy bonds, foreign currencies or even commodities within your portfolio.

The last type of mutual fund is called a "Fund of Funds" which means that it contains different types of mutual funds. When investing in a fund of funds you should look for one that has several different types of funds so that your money is protected against poor performance in one specific fund or index.

Once you have decided to invest in an index fund or mutual fund then the easiest way to purchase shares would be through the company directly since they will charge you less fees. However, if you don't have enough money to make a direct investment then there is another way to invest. You can always start with a small amount of money and then reinvest the gains from your initial investment in the same mutual fund.

If you are just starting out in the stock market it is important that you do not buy an index fund or mutual fund without knowing what it does. Every mutual fund will usually have a prospectus which explains everything about that specific index fund or mutual fund. If there are any questions about the fund, then you should follow up with a phone call to the company.

Chapter 11: Exchange Traded Funds (ETFs)

There has been a lot of buzz around ETFs in the media lately. You may have read, for instance, that they can offer diversification and lower costs. And that's true - but it's not the whole story! ETFs are investment funds that track an index, commodity or other benchmark. They trade like stocks on an exchange and seek to match their performance without any added management fees-making them a great option for individual investors who want to minimize trading costs. But similar to most investment vehicles, ETFs have some unique pros and cons. Here's what investors should know to make educated decisions about whether these funds are right for them.

What Makes an ETF Different?

ETFs aren't mutual funds or other types of managed products such as exchange-traded notes (ETNs). They're structured to track a particular investment benchmark instead of seeking to outperform it. For example, an ETF may hold stocks or bonds that are included in the S&P 500 index. Another way to think about it is that benchmarks usually represent a diversified basket of securities within a particular category and are generally calculated and maintained by third parties such as an index provider (e.g. MSCI, the Federal Reserve, etc.)

For example; an ETF might hold a handful of stocks it believes to be representative of the S&P 500 index, or even all 500 stocks. It only seeks to match what the index has done during the prior trading day by providing investors with an intraday return equal to that of the benchmark on a given day.

So What's in an ETF?

ETFs are generally structured as unit investment trusts (UITs), which means they're open-ended and ongoing vehicles that issue redeemable shares. They can invest in anything from equities and bonds to metals and commodities. They're also passively managed and their portfolios are valued daily because they're traded on an exchange. Some ETFs even provide the ability to short specific securities or indexes, giving investors more flexibility.

Exchange Traded Funds are a type of mutual fund that can be traded like stocks. It's an investment that provides diversified exposure to assets such as stocks, bonds, or commodities.

There are many ETFs and they come in different shapes and sizes with various strategies, which means it may take some time to figure out what you're looking for.

1. - Index ETFs

Index ETFs passively track an underlying index. For example, the Standard and Poor's 500 Index, which is comprised of the largest companies in the US market by market capitalization listed on the NYSE or NASDAQ.

When you invest in an index ETF, you're investing in a basket of securities representing that particular index. Therefore, if your investment goes up then it's because your underlying basket did well too whether it's based on investable indexes such as bond indexes or non-investable indexes such as commodity indexes.

2. - ETFs that aim to track a specific index and outperform it

These ETFs hold the underlying securities in the same proportion as they appear in the index, but they are designed to outperform it. This means that if, for example, you're expecting a large capital gain in a particular sector then you'd want to buy an ETF that aims to track the benchmark but with less volatility. For example, you might invest in an ETF that tracks the S&P 500 Index but invests 75% of its holdings in stocks with above average fundamentals such as high earnings growth and low debt.

3. - Sector funds – US based indexes

These aim to track a specific sector such as technology or health care. If you're looking to invest in a specific sector, then you might want to consider an ETF that bets on one of these sectors.

4. - Broadly diversified ETFs

These are similar to index ETFs and hold a basket of assets and track the index but have a broader spectrum of holdings. While this means more diversification it also means less individual stock research is required. An investor who doesn't want to spend much time monitoring his investments may prefer this type of fund.

5. - Managed ETFs

These are actively managed ETFs. They require the work of an investment manager to oversee their holdings and are not tied to a particular index.

In summary, if you're looking for a simple way to invest in stocks and bonds then consider using an ETF; however, be sure to do your research before making any final decisions about which type of ETF is right for you and, perhaps more importantly, how to buy them. As the number of Exchange Traded Funds increases so does the number of ways for investors to trade them, including direct access trading as well as traditional brokers and advisors.

It is also possible to trade an ETF in a tax-advantaged account such as a 401(k) or an IRA (using a Traditional or Roth IRA). This may allow for some tax advantages that would be unavailable from using other investment vehicles.

Apart from the bid-ask spread, investors should consider brokerage and transfer fees, which can vary depending on the selected trading platform. In addition, additional fees may apply when investing in specific ETFs. For example, some types of ETFs have higher per-trade commissions than others.

Also, if an investor plans to trade frequently or reinvest his dividends (a common strategy) he could incur significant transaction costs in a short period of time if he chooses to use a brokerage firm that offers low trading commissions for individual trades.

ETFs can be held alongside other investments such as mutual funds or stocks. This makes them useful in constructing a well-rounded portfolio that offers diversification and liquidity to investors. However, not all ETFs can be freely bought and sold in an investor's brokerage account. Those that are listed on exchanges must meet certain requirements and therefore have more liquidity than others, which may only be available to trade via order book at major brokerage houses (for example, Guggenheim S&P 500 Equal Weight ETF (RSP)).

Other widely traded U.S. ETFs include the iShares Core S&P Mid-Cap ETF (IJH), which tracks the S&P MidCap

400 index, and the iShares Russell 2000 ETF (IWM), which tracks the Russell 2000 Index.

ETFs may appeal to certain investors who want to invest in a specific sector or country, but lack sufficient capital or time to build a portfolio of individual securities. By using an ETF, an investor can quickly assemble a diverse basket of securities that track specific markets such as oil and gas drilling companies or an entire nation's stock market.

ETFs have been around for almost two decades and they are quickly becoming mainstream. In fact, ETFs now represent one of the most important financial investment products in the marketplace.

Some investors use ETFs as a way to gain exposure to different securities such as commodities, stocks or bonds -- all with just one trade. An investor may want exposure to a particular industry sector but does not want the risk that comes with individual stock ownership. The investor can purchase an index-based ETF that tracks a specific group of securities providing diversification benefits in this manner.

While there are many different ETFs out there, they can be grouped into three main categories:

1) Equity ETFs; 2) Fixed Income ETFs; and 3) Commodity ETFs. Within each of these categories are numerous sub-categories. Here's a sampling:

Equity ETFs

Global Equity (including emerging markets)

Large Cap Value (e.g., iShares S&P 500 Value Index Fund)

Mid Cap (e.g., iShares S&P MidCap Index Fund)

Small Cap (e.g., iShares Russell 2000 Index Fund)

Industrials (e.g. Power Shares Dynamic Industrials Portfolio)

Real Estate (e.g., Market Vectors Retail REIT ETF)

Fixed Income ETFs

US treasury (e.g., iShares iBoxx T-Bond Index Fund) - This is a good way to play the changing interest rate environment.

High Yield (e.g., Direxion Daily 20+ Year Treasury Bear 3X Shares) - This is a good way to play the credit markets including financial stocks.

Municipal Bonds (e.g. iShares S&P National AMT-Free Muni Bond Index Fund)- This is a good way to play the municipal bond market.

Commodity ETFs

Energy (e.g., Market Vectors Oil Refiners ETF) - This is a good way to play the energy sector.

Precious Metals (e.g., SPDR Gold Shares) - This is a good way to play the precious metal sector.

Agriculture (e.g., Power Shares DB Agriculture Fund) -- This is a good way to play the agriculture sector.

As one can see, ETFs can be used in numerous ways for a variety of purposes. The question is: When should one buy or sell an ETF?

The general consensus is that if an individual investor would like to invest in the stock market but does not want to actually buy and sell stocks outright, then an ETF product may be the right investment vehicle. Likewise, if someone wants exposure to commodities -- but do not want to actually buy and sell physical gold, silver or soybeans -- then a commodity ETF will provide this type of exposure.

If you are buying a particular ETF for the long-term and mean to keep it there until you need your money, then you can hold on until retirement. On the other hand, if you plan to trade more actively and have the time to do so, then there may be times when you should buy and sell ETFs.

For example, if stock markets enter a prolonged down cycle, an investor may decide to get out there and buy stocks at these lower levels after a correction in order to replace those stocks that are now underperforming their benchmarks. At such a time, selling their ETF shares and buying individual stocks would provide this type of exposure. There was one particular individual who bought shares in a small-cap value ETF against the advice of many Wall Street professionals. He held his position during the 2008 market crash and today is one of the most over-leveraged, but also one of the most profitable investors out there.

Conversely, if markets are going up for an extended period of time as they have been in recent years, an ETF investor may decide to get out there and sell their holdings in order to take profits. Again, selling their shares and buying individual stocks would provide such exposure. In recent years we have seen many investors who sold their holdings of small-cap value ETFs in order to buy large-cap value stocks (e.g., iShares Russell 2000 Value Index Fund vs iShares S&P 500 Value Index Fund). While this strategy is a great way to hedge one's bet, it is not advisable to make such drastic changes all at once.

While there are several risks and complexities associated with investing in ETFs, individuals who take the time to educate themselves on what they are buying should be able to avoid some of the pitfalls. What is important is that investors in ETFs remember that these investments are not immune to extreme downward changes just because they may have done well over the long term.

Chapter 12: Other Types of Investments

Cryptocurrencies

Cryptocurrencies are a medium of exchange using cryptography to secure transactions, control the creation of additional units, and authenticate the transfer of assets. Cryptocurrencies let buyers and sellers conduct financial transactions without revealing their identities. By decentralizing public transaction data, cryptocurrencies eliminate the need for third-party checking and verification. The first cryptocurrency to capture popular attention was Bitcoin, which was launched in 2009 by an individual or group operating under the name Satoshi Nakamoto. Like other currencies, Bitcoins are not backed by a physical commodity but rather by a peer-to-peer network of computers users who use the coins as money.

What is bitcoin?

Bitcoin was introduced on 31 October 2008 to a cryptography mailing list, and released as open-source software in 2009. It is a cryptocurrency, so-called because it uses cryptography to control the creation of its units of currency and verify the transfer of assets. Bitcoin transactions are irreversible and immune to fraudulent chargebacks. The system is peer-to-peer and transactions take place between users directly through the use of cryptography.

The Bitcoin market is an important space that has been sending traders scrambling in search of a reliable exchange platform. If you want to invest in cryptocurrencies, then there are five exchanges on which you can do so: Coinbase, Bit stamp, Kraken, Bitfinex and Poloniex.

You may not be familiar with all of these platforms as they tend to cater to more tech-savvy traders. What's interesting about each is that they vary in their approach to how you buy and sell cryptocurrencies--in other words what currencies they offer and how advanced their trading infrastructure is.

Gold and Silver

Investing in physical gold and silver is a tangible, proven strategy to hedge against economic uncertainty. It can't be stolen like the cash in your bank account, and it doesn't need an internet connection to retain its value. Gold and silver are liquid assets that can be conveniently transformed into cash at any time, with no restrictive holding periods or costs.

In recent weeks the prices of both precious metals have been climbing steadily upwards, with talk of inflation creeping back into conversations around financial markets. Today gold is up $10.80 an ounce at $1,633, and silver is up $0.32 an ounce at $36.27, prices are climbing steadily higher in 2017.

Many people put off purchasing physical gold or silver because they feel it's a complicated process that requires significant research or expertise, but the truth is that you don't need any special skills or training to get started investing in physical gold and silver.

Gold is primarily an investment whereas silver is primarily industrial. Quite simply, gold has a far greater store of value as a raw commodity than silver does. However, because it's primarily an investment rather than an industrial metal, it can experience swings in price more dramatically than the price fluctuations experienced by silver which is used more for practical purposes such as jewelry or in medicine.

If you want a quick turnaround, buying gold or silver bullion coins or bars is not advised because it takes two weeks or longer for delivery after purchase if purchased through most dealers. Precious metals can also be stored with certain non-bank storage facilities, but lockups are not insured.

Precious metals purchased through your brokerage account with a bank or credit union may be covered by the Federal Deposit Insurance Corp., but check with the company first. Insurance payouts can take up to 60 days; the metal itself is typically received in three days.

Private Equity

Private equity has been around since the 1970s, but for some reason these days it's getting a lot of attention. Private equity is a type of investment fund that uses investors' money to buy companies.

Private equity is a pretty straight-forward concept.

A private equity fund is almost exactly the same as any other investment fund (like a mutual fund or hedge fund) -- it just invests in a slightly different type of investment.

As with other types of funds, private equity funds will be bought and sold on stock exchanges. You can use exchange-traded funds (ETFs) to invest in large private equity firms like Blackstone and TPG Capital. For traders, the ETFs for Blackstone and TPG Capital are BXLT and TPLM, respectively.

. For example, Marriott, Hyatt and Hilton are all owned by private equity firms like Blackstone.

The biggest drawback to private equity investing is that it's a lot riskier.

If you're invested in a mutual fund that owns stock, the worst-case scenario is a complete loss of your investment -- but this would be extremely rare because most companies don't go completely bankrupt.

In contrast, private equity funds can lose all of their money and often times will.

And even though private equity funds are a type of investment fund and have the same risk/reward characteristic as other types of investment funds, they are taxed differently.

Rather than being taxed only when you sell your investment (like mutual funds), private equity is taxed on a yearly basis -- the amount invested plus profit is considered income each year.

Hedge Funds

Hedge funds is an industry that deals in the regulation of investments and speculation. The hedge fund industry has experienced significant growth in recent years, with over 8,000 hedge funds managing about $3 trillion in assets as of December 2013. Hedge Funds, or funds of hedge funds, are investment vehicles that are made out of investments in other investment companies. The most common form of a hedge fund is a pooled investment vehicle with the goal to reduce risk by using an array of investments and trading strategies. Hedge funds have been used since 1954 and were created because conventional publicly traded securities were producing less than satisfactory returns.

The goal is to make as much money as possible while also ensuring that the investor does not lose any money on bad trades. A hedge fund manager is a person who earns money via performance fees, incentive compensation, and trading profits.

Ethical Investments

Ethical investing is a technique where an investor picks investments dependent on an individual ethical code. Ethical investing endeavors to help enterprises having a constructive outcome, for example, manageable energy, and make an investment return. With an increment in ESG assets, there are more ethical investments than any other time in recent memory.

Obviously, what is "ethical" relies upon the individual. What is ethical to you may not be to another person. That is the reason it's essential to look in the background of ethical investments and ensure they line up with the effect you'd prefer to have. While no investment is ensured, the exhibition of ethical assets has been demonstrated to be like the presentation of customary assets — truth be told, some exploration shows that ethical asset execution might be predominant. As indicated by Morningstar information, maintainable assets beat their conventional friends in 2019, with 66% completing the year with returns in the top portion of their Morningstar classes.

The overall thought is that organizations that treat their workers well and are smart about their natural effect may likewise be better run and less inclined to embarrassment — which can bring about a material advantage. For instance, organizations that cling to ESG concerns may stay away from fines and claims for issues, for example, botch of harmful material removal, rape and harassment charges and false exchanges, since they may have arrangements to help dodge those issues in any case.

There is likewise some proof that recommends that ethical assets may offer lower levels of market hazard than customary assets, even in unstable markets, for example, the plunge during the initial not many months of the COVID-19 pandemic. As indicated by Morningstar information, 24 out of 26 ESG list supports outflanked tantamount ordinary assets during the main quarter of 2020.

Coins, Stamps and Art

Coins

Coins are well-known investments, but they can often be hard to come by. One of the most popular ones for collectors is US pennies before the year 1982. Most will start at about $5 and increase at about 10% per year — depending on the date you buy one and when you sell it. Most people don't keep track of coins for their entire life, so when they're found in old furniture or wallets, the owner will sell them to a coin collector.

Stamps

Stamps are another collectible. They aren't as popular as coins or other collectibles because they're fairly easy to find, but, for stamps issued after 1989 (when they stopped using the mail system to sell them), you can expect an increase in value of about 10% per year.

Art

If you're in the mood to invest in something more artistic, then art might be just the thing. The timelessness of great works of art is legendary, so the investment potential is gigantic.

There are other reasons to invest in art, too. For example, if your home or office has a limited amount of wall space, buying an art piece will add value to the environment — and if you're not able to repay your loan on the art, then you can just sell it again later and recoup some of your losses.

Collectible coins can be a solid investment when done strategically. Stamps can also provide an interesting opportunity if you know how to buy and sell them effectively. Finally, art has always been viewed as one of the most lucrative investments out there, though many people don't see it as a realistic option for their budgets.

Chapter 13: Conclusion

Choosing suitable investments is not an easy decision, but it is essential to build a diverse portfolio and focus on diversification and long-term sustainability. In particular, it is crucial to identify the best formula based on your objectives, available capital, and risk/return ratio, making investments in line with the goals you want to achieve.

For example, you may favor low-risk assets to protect your capital while preceding a higher return, or you may accept higher risk in exchange for the prospect of a higher return. In any case, it is essential to protect capital adequately by considering ancillary factors such as costs, liquidity, early redemption, and management methods when selecting investments.

The important thing, in any case, is to keep the focus on risk management so that the assets in the portfolio can offer a return in line with one's needs and with a duration of investment suited to one's objectives, diversifying as much as possible to minimize risk.

With this handbook, I hope to have given you a clear and helpful map for moving within the complex investment world.

It is up to you to choose your path, but remember to act with caution, especially at the beginning. Do a lot of practice, inform yourself, and study.

www.ingramcontent.com/pod-product-compliance
Lightning Source LLC
Chambersburg PA
CBHW070745030726
47601CB00001B/147